Get stuff done.

Date:

Top priority

My notes

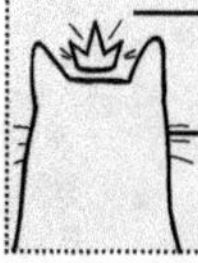

Date:

Top priority

My notes

Date:

Top priority

My notes

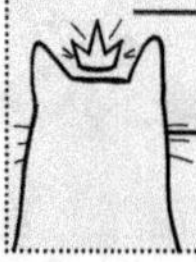

Date:

Top priority

My notes

Date:

Top priority

My notes

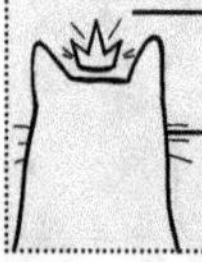

Date:

Top priority

My notes

Date:

Top priority

My notes

Date:

Top priority

My notes

Date:

Top priority

My notes

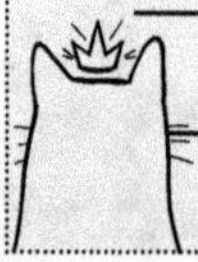

Date:

Top priority

My notes

Date:

Top priority

My notes

Date:

Top priority

My notes

Date:

Top priority

My notes

Date:

Top priority

My notes

Date:

Top priority

My notes

Date:

Top priority

My notes

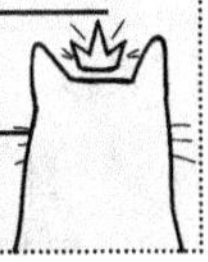

Date:

Top priority

My notes

Date:

Top priority

- [ ]
- [ ]
- [ ]

- [ ]
- [ ]
- [ ]
- [ ]
- [ ]
- [ ]
- [ ]
- [ ]
- [ ]
- [ ]
- [ ]
- [ ]
- [ ]
- [ ]
- [ ]
- [ ]
- [ ]

My notes

Date:

Top priority

- [ ]
- [ ]
- [ ]

- [ ]
- [ ]
- [ ]
- [ ]
- [ ]
- [ ]
- [ ]
- [ ]
- [ ]
- [ ]
- [ ]
- [ ]
- [ ]
- [ ]
- [ ]
- [ ]
- [ ]

My notes

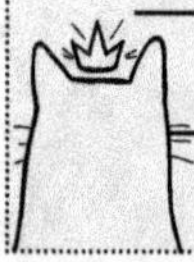

Date:

Top priority

My notes

Date:

Top priority

My notes

Date:

Top priority

- [ ]
- [ ]
- [ ]

- [ ]
- [ ]
- [ ]
- [ ]
- [ ]
- [ ]
- [ ]
- [ ]
- [ ]
- [ ]
- [ ]
- [ ]
- [ ]
- [ ]
- [ ]
- [ ]
- [ ]

My notes

Date:

Top priority

My notes

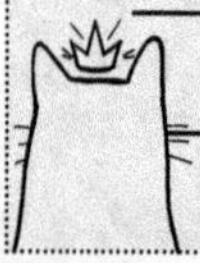

Date:

Top priority

My notes

Date:

Top priority

My notes

Date:

Top priority

My notes

Date:

Top priority

My notes

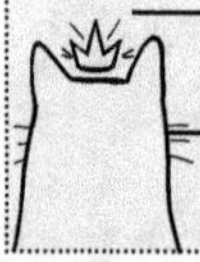

Date:

Top priority

My notes

Date:

Top priority

My notes

Date:

Top priority

My notes

Date:

Top priority

My notes

Date:

Top priority

My notes

Date:

Top priority

My notes

Date:

Top priority

My notes

Date:

Top priority

My notes

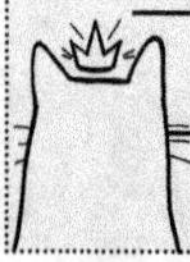

Date:

Top priority

My notes

Date:

Top priority

My notes

Date:

Top priority

My notes

Date:

Top priority

My notes

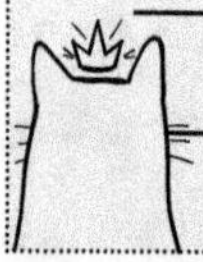

Date:

Top priority

My notes

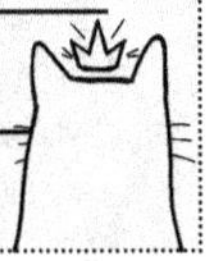

Date:

Top priority

- [ ]
- [ ]
- [ ]

- [ ]
- [ ]
- [ ]
- [ ]
- [ ]
- [ ]
- [ ]
- [ ]
- [ ]
- [ ]
- [ ]
- [ ]
- [ ]
- [ ]
- [ ]
- [ ]
- [ ]

My notes

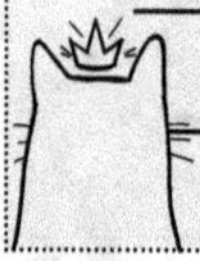

Date:

Top priority

My notes

Date:

Top priority

My notes

Date:

Top priority

My notes

Date:

Top priority

My notes

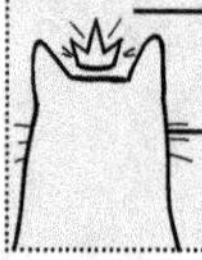

Date:

Top priority

My notes

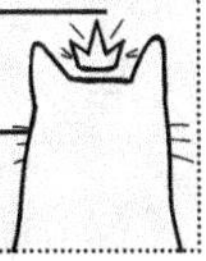

Date:

Top priority

- [ ]
- [ ]
- [ ]

- [ ]
- [ ]
- [ ]
- [ ]
- [ ]
- [ ]
- [ ]
- [ ]
- [ ]
- [ ]
- [ ]
- [ ]
- [ ]
- [ ]
- [ ]
- [ ]
- [ ]

My notes

Date:

Top priority

My notes

Date:

Top priority

My notes

Date:

Top priority

My notes

Date:

Top priority

My notes

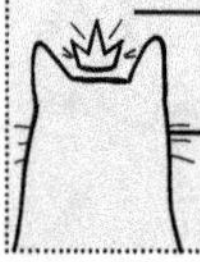

Date:

Top priority

- [ ]
- [ ]
- [ ]

- [ ]
- [ ]
- [ ]
- [ ]
- [ ]
- [ ]
- [ ]
- [ ]
- [ ]
- [ ]
- [ ]
- [ ]
- [ ]
- [ ]
- [ ]
- [ ]
- [ ]

My notes

Date:

Top priority

- [ ]
- [ ]
- [ ]

- [ ]
- [ ]
- [ ]
- [ ]
- [ ]
- [ ]
- [ ]
- [ ]
- [ ]
- [ ]
- [ ]
- [ ]
- [ ]
- [ ]
- [ ]
- [ ]
- [ ]

My notes

Date:

Top priority

My notes

Date:

Top priority

My notes

Date:

Top priority

My notes

Date:

Top priority

My notes

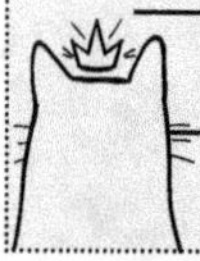

Date:

Top priority

My notes

Date:

Top priority

My notes

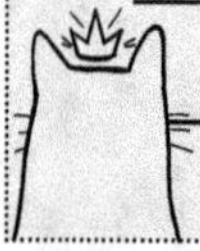

Date:

Top priority

- [ ]
- [ ]
- [ ]

- [ ]
- [ ]
- [ ]
- [ ]
- [ ]
- [ ]
- [ ]
- [ ]
- [ ]
- [ ]
- [ ]
- [ ]
- [ ]
- [ ]
- [ ]
- [ ]
- [ ]

My notes

Date:

Top priority

- [ ]
- [ ]
- [ ]

- [ ]
- [ ]
- [ ]
- [ ]
- [ ]
- [ ]
- [ ]
- [ ]
- [ ]
- [ ]
- [ ]
- [ ]
- [ ]
- [ ]
- [ ]
- [ ]
- [ ]

My notes

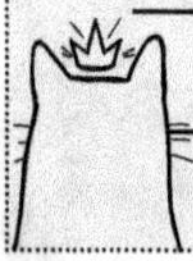

Date:

Top priority

My notes

Date:

Top priority

My notes

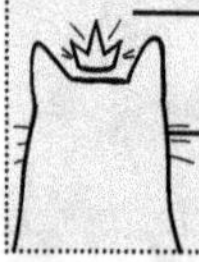

Date:

Top priority

My notes

Date:

Top priority

My notes

Date:

Top priority

My notes

Date:

Top priority

My notes

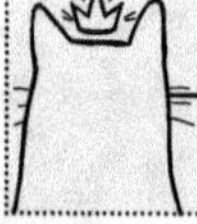

Date:

Top priority

My notes

Date:

Top priority

- [ ]
- [ ]
- [ ]

- [ ]
- [ ]
- [ ]
- [ ]
- [ ]
- [ ]
- [ ]
- [ ]
- [ ]
- [ ]
- [ ]
- [ ]
- [ ]
- [ ]
- [ ]
- [ ]
- [ ]

My notes

Date:

Top priority

My notes

Date:

Top priority

My notes

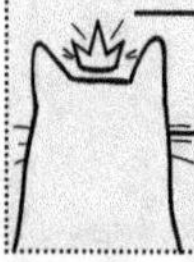

Date:

Top priority

My notes

Date:

Top priority

My notes

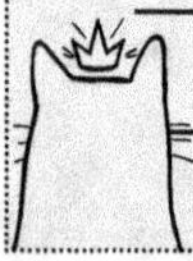

Date:

Top priority

My notes

Date:

Top priority

My notes

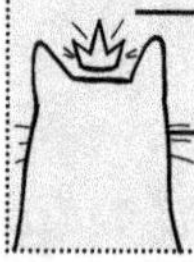

Date:

Top priority

My notes

Date:

Top priority

☐
☐
☐

☐
☐
☐
☐
☐
☐
☐
☐
☐
☐
☐
☐
☐
☐
☐
☐
☐

My notes

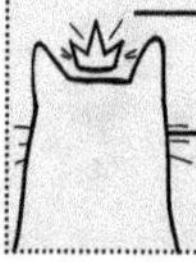

Date:

Top priority

My notes

Date:

Top priority

My notes

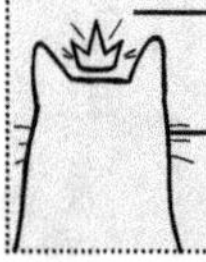

Date:

Top priority

My notes

Date:

Top priority

My notes

Date:

Top priority

My notes

Date:

Top priority

- [ ]
- [ ]
- [ ]

- [ ]
- [ ]
- [ ]
- [ ]
- [ ]
- [ ]
- [ ]
- [ ]
- [ ]
- [ ]
- [ ]
- [ ]
- [ ]
- [ ]
- [ ]
- [ ]
- [ ]

My notes

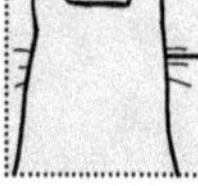

Date:

Top priority

My notes

Date:

Top priority

My notes

Date:

Top priority

- [ ]
- [ ]
- [ ]

- [ ]
- [ ]
- [ ]
- [ ]
- [ ]
- [ ]
- [ ]
- [ ]
- [ ]
- [ ]
- [ ]
- [ ]
- [ ]
- [ ]
- [ ]
- [ ]
- [ ]

My notes

Date:

Top priority

My notes

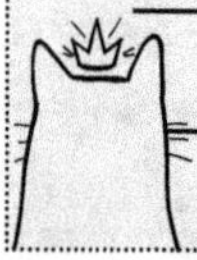

Date:

Top priority

My notes

Date:

Top priority

My notes

Date:

Top priority

- [ ]
- [ ]
- [ ]

- [ ]
- [ ]
- [ ]
- [ ]
- [ ]
- [ ]
- [ ]
- [ ]
- [ ]
- [ ]
- [ ]
- [ ]
- [ ]
- [ ]
- [ ]
- [ ]
- [ ]

My notes

Date:

Top priority

My notes

Date:

Top priority

My notes

Date:

Top priority

My notes

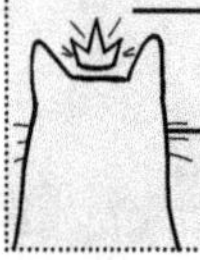

Date:

Top priority

My notes

Date:

Top priority

My notes

Date:

Top priority

My notes

Date:

Top priority

My notes

Date:

Top priority

My notes

Date:

Top priority

My notes

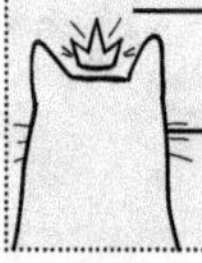

Date:

Top priority

My notes

Date:

Top priority

My notes

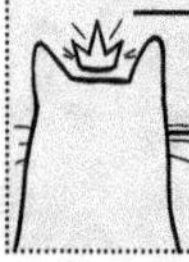

Date:

Top priority

My notes

Date:

Top priority

My notes

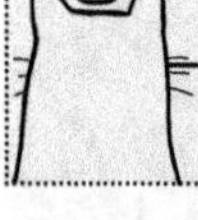

Date:

Top priority

My notes

Date:

Top priority

My notes

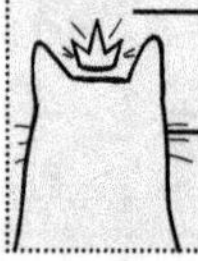

Date:

Top priority

- [ ]
- [ ]
- [ ]

- [ ]
- [ ]
- [ ]
- [ ]
- [ ]
- [ ]
- [ ]
- [ ]
- [ ]
- [ ]
- [ ]
- [ ]
- [ ]
- [ ]
- [ ]
- [ ]
- [ ]

My notes

Date:

Top priority

My notes

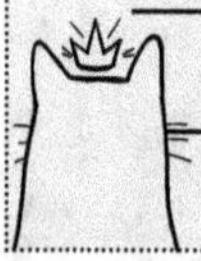

Date:

Top priority

My notes

Date:

Top priority

My notes

Date:

Top priority

My notes

Date:

Top priority

My notes

Date:

Top priority

My notes

Date:

Top priority

My notes

Date:

Top priority

- [ ]
- [ ]
- [ ]

- [ ]
- [ ]
- [ ]
- [ ]
- [ ]
- [ ]
- [ ]
- [ ]
- [ ]
- [ ]
- [ ]
- [ ]
- [ ]
- [ ]
- [ ]
- [ ]
- [ ]

My notes

Date:

Top priority

My notes

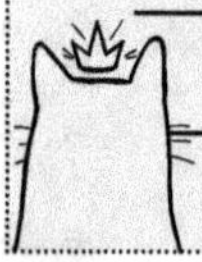

Date:

Top priority

My notes

Date:

Top priority

My notes

Date:

Top priority

- [ ] ______
- [ ] ______
- [ ] ______

- [ ] ______
- [ ] ______
- [ ] ______
- [ ] ______
- [ ] ______
- [ ] ______
- [ ] ______
- [ ] ______
- [ ] ______
- [ ] ______
- [ ] ______
- [ ] ______
- [ ] ______
- [ ] ______
- [ ] ______
- [ ] ______
- [ ] ______

My notes

______

______

______

Date:

Top priority

My notes

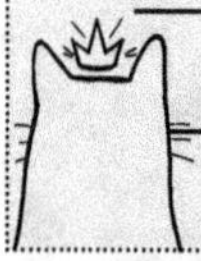

Date:

Top priority

My notes

www.ingramcontent.com/pod-product-compliance
Lightning Source LLC
Chambersburg PA
CBHW051319220526
45468CB00004B/1412
9781796253580